Buckaroo Poetry

Cowboy Poems for Young and Old

by P.W. Conway

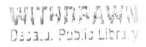
Buckaroo Poetry
Cowboy Poems for Young and Old
Original cowboy poetry by P.W. Conway
aka "Cactus Pete"

ISBN- 13: 978-1481884518

Book cover, design, illustrations and graphic layouts by
Carolyn Valdez Phillips

Please visit the author's websites at
Buckaroopoetry.com
Pwconway.com

Blue Cactus Publishing
Simi Valley, CA

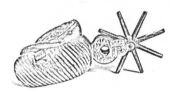

Dedication

To the love of my life, my wife Maria, who for so many years, has put up with the little buckaroo in me.

Buckaroo Poetry

Table of Contents

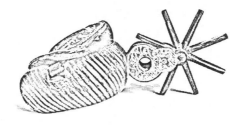

Foreword

The West is not only a place, but a state of mind. The West may be faded but will never disappear as long as there are American men who stand on their own two feet, face problems straight in the eye, never back down and never give in. They may be scared, but saddle up anyway.

Cowboy poetry fits the man of the open West. A good poem is short, sweet and straight to the point. With just a few well-chosen words, volumes are said.

Peter Conway has brought us to this magical place through his Buckaroo Poetry that speaks of cowboys, horses, ranching and the wonderful West.

Thanks, Peter. I've enjoyed your works and am sure other westerners will see themselves in your stories.

Peter Sherayko
Actor, Author

Acknowledgments

Thanks to my good friend, actor Peter Sherayko, who played Texas Jack Vermillion in the film "Tombstone," for his kind words. Peter Sherayko is also a renowned author of several books, including <u>Tombstone: The Guns and Gear</u> and his new book, <u>The Fringe of Hollywood, The Art of Making a Western</u>.

A big buckaroo thank you to Steven Sanchez, CEO of IN-EXUS.com. Without his help and guidance I would still be reciting poetry to my horse in his corral.

The back cover photograph was taken by my friend and world famous artist, Morgan Weistling. You can also see Mr. Weistling's work on permanent display at the Cowboy Hall of Fame in Oklahoma and the Autry National Heritage Museum in California. Please see his amazing art at http://www.morganweistling.net.

I would like to thank Georgia Trumble, Karla Hubbell, Pat Havens and Wayne Ferber for their assistance and support. Their ongoing efforts and dedication to the preservation of history in the Conejo Valley are keeping the early days of ranching alive in Simi Valley, California.

Thank you to all of my friends at the Strathearn Historical Park and Museum, who have encouraged me to write and recite my cowboy poetry. A special thanks to Carol Thomaier, Gail McVicker, Heather McDaniel, Linda Arcari, Laura Jean Hole and Stephanie Lapeyre, who have put up with my endless tales and stories of the old west.

To ranchers Tom and Charlotte Crocker, for their ongoing support of cowboy poetry and the cowboy culture.

My deepest appreciation to Carolyn Valdez Phillips. Without her tireless effort in putting this volume together, <u>Buckaroo Poetry</u> would just be another one of "tomorrow's" projects.

Ol' 519

I'm a pretty good old cowboy.
I can ride and rope some too.
But there was just one thing, I ain't never done,
That I always wanted to do.

As a young buckaroo I never forgot,
The first time I saw the show.
From that day on, I always wanted
to ride in the rodeo.

I saw them boys on saddle broncs
A leap'n for the sky.
And I knew right then, there'd come a day,
When I would have to try.

I saw a cowboy leap from his horse
And bring a steer down to the ground.
And many a time I wondered,
If I could take one down.

I've seen a lot of rides and wrecks,
The best cowboys come and go.
And still I wondered deep inside,
If I could rodeo.

Well, the years went by and I figured out
That I was run'n out of time.
And I'd best just get'r done
Before I'm past my prime.

So I set my mind and packed my gear,
It was time to take a chance
And look up Mr. Billy T,
At the Buck'n T Bar Ranch.

Ol' Billy T had been a rodeo clown
And a bullfighter extraordinaire,
But he took to raising rough stock
For the rodeos and county fair.

Well, I told him of my schemes and dreams
Since that day I was a boy,
About riding in a rodeo,
It'd be my greatest joy.

He asked, are ya sure you want to do this?
'Cause if you really do,
Yur gonna have to cowboy up,
'Cause I got just the bull for you.

Ol' 519, he's been around
And he's as tricky as they come.
But if you think you can handle him,
You can ride him just for fun.

Now I know that you ride horses
And you can cowboy pretty fair.
But ride'n bulls is another thing,
But I'll let ya if ya dare.

I thought to myself as I swallowed hard,
It's time to do or die.
So I looked Billy T right in his eyes
And said, I'll give that bull a try.

They brought him out, ol' 519
And ran him in the chutes.
Billy handed me some spurs
And had me strap 'em to my boots.

I took a breath and climbed the gate
And set down nice and slow.
And Billy said before you ride
There's a few things you should know.

Keep yur toes a pointed out
And press them heels in tight.
You let yur free arm balance you,
It will keep you centered right.

He'll come out buck'n to the left,
Then turn back into your hand.
But you just slide yur backside
To where you think he's gonna land.

Just ride him hard and don't look down,
Or you'll end up in the dirt.
It ain't the ride that's painful,
It's the get off that will hurt.

4

I swallowed hard and yelled let'r buck.
The gate it swung out wide.
I couldn't catch my breath at all,
No matter how I tried.

He started jumping a little bit,
Well, a crow hop some might say.
He tried to get me off his back,
But this was gonna be my day.

My free arm flopp'n all around,
My hat flew from my head.
I knew it weren't too pretty,
But at least I wasn't dead.

He was a twist'n a little to the left,
Then turned back the other way.
He started pick'n up the pace,
But I was ready for the fray.

I guess he'd finally had enough
And he put me on the ground.
I landed pretty hard and
It made an ugly sound.

I saw him turn towards me,
He was big and mean and black.
My heart was in my throat,
As I laid there on my back.

He bent his head down close to me,
I could smell his evil breath.
I saw them black eyes staring down,
I knew I was face'n death.

He gave a snort and scuffed his hoof
And I believe I started to pray.
Then that ol' bull just licked my face
And turned and walked away.

Now Billy T was laugh'n hard
And all the boys was a pokin' fun.
That ol' bull's name was Tinkerbell
And he was as gentle as they come.

But to me he'll always be ol' 519,
The baddest of the bad.
The meanest bull that ever was,
The greatest ride I ever had.

Wanda Jean and Me

We just kind a found each other,
Me and Wanda Jean.
We was both a little lost
And I reckon both a little mean.

We was both a little barn sour,
Been penned up way too long.
With out no real direction,
A critter can just go wrong.

The very first time I saddled her up,
She jerked me to the ground.
The second time, I held my own
Until she settled down.

We'd both been down some pretty rough trail,
Ol' Wanda Jean and me.
But it weren't long before we figured out,
That we was meant to be.

We'd cross them creeks and climb them hills
Just to see the other side.
Then gaze upon what God had made
And be filled with humble pride.

We'd ride those trails from dawn to dusk
And chase some cows along the way.
Then bunk beneath a twisted tree,
Until the night became the day.

I'd sit there by the fire
And tell her of my schemes.
The ones that'd never happen
And all the broken dreams.

She'd just keep eat'n that fresh green grass
And whinny now and then.
With big brown eyes a shine'n bright,
That ol' girl was my best friend.

As time went by, we rested more,
Her trot had slowed way down.
And it seemed to me those stirrups
Were get'n further from the ground.

She was get'n a little long in the tooth
And my hair was a turning gray.
But we both still had a few trails left,
Before we called it a day.

In time we trailed on flatter ground,
Her flanks were a get'n thin.
I'd rub her ears and reminisce
About the places we had been.

About the sunsets on the mountain
And all the beauty that we'd seen.
We had ourselves a time,
Me and Wanda Jean.

She closed her eyes for the very last time
Beneath that twisted tree.
Many a day it shaded us,
Ol' Wanda Jean and me.

I laid my head down by the fire
And drifted off to sleep.
I dreamt of all them times we had
And the memories I'd keep.

I saw us head'n down the trail,
We were young and strong and free.
I know we'll ride again someday.
Ol' Wanda Jean and me.

The Horse Whisperer

I saw this here program on TV
About a man who talks to his horse.
He whispers in the softest voice
And that horse listens up of course.

He said ya don't want to hurt his feelings,
You must be the sensitive one.
And for God sake, don't let him know he's a horse
And that there's ranch work to be done.

Tell your horse he's your very best friend
And let him know just how much you care.
Be sure to rub his ears and give'm a hug
And he'll follow you anywhere.

Now I can do the same thing with a carrot
Or a big ol' bucket of grain.
Then work that horse in summer heat
Or push cows in a pouring rain.

But I was will'n to listen
To this horse talking fellow again.
But I couldn't believe my eyes and ears
When that horse started talk'n back to him.

That ol' boy whispered someth'n,
Then leaned back and chuckled out loud.
And that horse tossed his head and whinnied
And got a big laugh from the crowd.

Now I learned ranch'n from my daddy
And he learned the very same way.
I can't believe we've been doing it wrong
Until this very day.

I surely wish I had the time
To mosey out to the corral
And sit and sip my coffee
And have a biscuit with my pal.

I don't know if I'll ever
Share a long neck with my mount,
Or get him to laugh at my jokes,
Or even teach him how to count.

Now I'm in a quandary
Figurin' whatever should be done.
Do I tell him this is a day spa
And we're here to have some fun?

I tried to whisper in his ear
And he just twitched and pulled away.
He really didn't give a darn
About what I had to say.

Well, I've had enough of this I thought,
It's time to get back to work.
So I threw my saddle on his back
And grabbed my rope and quirt.

I tried to be a horse whisperer,
But he wouldn't listen, and so,
Now we're back to working cows
And doing what we know.

But I do have a whole new respect
For this equine friend of mine.
He taught me ya can't be what you're not
And I reckon that's just fine.

So I'll keep on being a cowboy
And he'll keep on being a horse
And we'll leave the whisper'n to young lovers
And go back to work'n cattle of course.

The Old Man's Ranch

I parked my truck behind the barn
And made my way towards the house.
As I was walk'n up the path
I saw the old man and his spouse.

He sat up there upon his porch,
His hands were old and weathered.
His face was grizzled by the sun,
It looked like saddle leather.

His fists, they clenched the rocking chair
As it moved slowly to and fro.
Behind his blurry eyes were memories
That he may never know.

I could tell that he was staring
At something far away.
It could have been his past
Or the distant fields of hay.

I wondered what he saw out there,
Was it another place and time?
Or just a water colored image
That made no sense or rhyme.

The woman sitting next to him
Got up to go inside.
She smiled as she brushed away
A tear she tried to hide.

He strained his eyes and looked at me,
I know he wondered who I was.
And the expression on his face
Was enough to give me pause.

I said my name is Robert.
He said my name's Robert too.
He stuck out that ol' weathered hand
And said how do you do.

Do I know you, young fella?
Have you been this way before?
I said, yes sir a time or two
To help out with the chores.

I wanted him to talk to me,
So I looked at him and said,
Why don't you tell me what it's like
Out here on your spread?

He said, why we're all ranch'n folks,
Are you a rancher too?
I said I've worked my share of cows,
But not near as much as you.

He said, I ain't sure just how I started,
I really can't recall,
But, I've been ranch'n all my life
And I guess I've done it all.

A cowboy's life ain't easy.
It's hard and lonely too.
It takes every ounce of strength you got
Just to do what you got to do.

And just when you can catch your breath,
And ya think the chores are done,
Ya realize there's more work to do
Before the set'n of the sun.

Cowboy'n ain't for the weak of heart,
Or for them that ain't got try.
You just can't quit and walk away
You'll keep ranch'n 'til ya die.

Did I mention I'm a rancher?
Up here that's what we do.
I said, yes sir you did
And I'm a rancher too.

I guess that it don't matter
I'm forgetful now and then.
I'm proud ya came on by,
I hope ya stop this way again.

I'd like to sit and visit,
But I've got work to do.
This ol' place don't run itself,
So I'll say good day to you.

He just went back to stare'n out
With his little sheepish grin.
I wondered if he'd recall
This time I spent with him.

I knew I had to walk away,
And it made me kind of sad.
I turned my back and whispered,
Ya know, I love you dad.

Buckaroo Heaven

When I was just a little sprout
On my Daddy's ranch back home,
There were days when I would saddle up
And take off on my own.

I had this little pony,
Patches was his name.
He and I would cowboy
Until the winter rains.

We would head on down the road apiece
And take a left at Johnson's Bend,
Then lope across the meadow
Until we found the trail again.

Through the tree line and up the hill
Until we reached the very top,
There stood a run down cabin
And right there's where we'd stop.

Up atop of that ol' mountain
Were some cow pens made of wood
And a pile of rotting lumber
Where a little barn once stood.

There was this old time cowboy
That's what people said.
His name was Mr. Wheeler,
But most folks called him ol' Ned.

His beard was gray, like campfire smoke
And his eyes were dark like coal.
He looked like he'd been through hard times,
But he had a gentle soul.

He had a few ol' scrawny cows.
They just wandered here and there.
And just like that ol' cowboy,
They didn't seem to have a care.

Whenever me and Patches
Came a riding up the hill,
There he'd be a horse back,
Like a statue he was still.

I'd pull up right beside him
And he'd say howdy buckaroo.
I'd doff my hat and smile
And I'd say howdy too.

He'd tell me of the old days
Out there on the trails,
When there were such things as cowboys
Driv'n herds up to the rails.

Talk'n of the hardships,
The good times and the bad.
Sometimes he'd be smil'n
And sometimes he'd be sad.

Then he'd just stop talk'n
And stare off into space.
I could see it in his eyes,
He was in another time and place.

Whatever are you think'n of?
I finally asked ol' Ned.
He looked at me and smiled
And this is what he said.

There's a trail head up beyond the clouds,
A trail I'm gonna blaze,
A trail that leads to heaven
One of these fine days.

There'll come a time when the days're too hot
Or the nights get to dern cold,
And I'll saddle up and ride that trail.
I hear it's paved with gold.

The longhorns, they'll be a graz'n
And it will be springtime every day,
With the sun a shining up above
And the smell of fresh cut hay.

There'll be knee high grassy meadows
And a sing'n mountain stream.
It's called buckaroo heaven, sure enough
And it's a cowboy's dream.

Do you believe in heaven, son?
I said, you bet I do,
But I'm not sure I picture it
Exactly like you do.

24

He said, it's all about believing
In the things that we can't see,
Like springtime when it's snowin'
Or that seed that becomes the tree.

Well, I grew up and left the ranch
And struck out on my own.
Got myself a city job
Far from my boyhood home.

I went back home to see the folks,
They said ol' Ned had died.
So I saddled up a ranch horse
And went for one last ride.

I headed down the road apiece
Until I got to Johnson's Bend.
Through the meadow and up the hill,
It was like I was a kid again.

I rode hell bent for leather
'Til I reached the top of that ol' hill,
Then just sat there kind of quiet,
I can hear the silence still.

The cabin, it was all run down
And the brush was over grown.
It seemed like all the life was gone
And I was out there on my own.

Then I saw a deer break from the trees
And a hawk fly overhead.
Then look'n up at heaven
I doffed my hat towards ol' Ned.

Hello old friend, I whispered,
As I began to smile.
I just came up to say hello
And visit for awhile.

It's me, the little buckaroo
And I know it's been some time.
I'm grown up now and on my own
And yes, I'm doing fine.

I really miss your stories
Of the old days way back when,
Of dusty trails and campfires
And the cattle drives, old friend.

Now I tell my own kids
Of a cowboy I used to know
Who could drive a herd of longhorns
Through summer heat or winter snow.

A man who worked hard every day
And never once complained.
He'd just saddle up and do his job
And took life as it came.

A man who taught me the little things
That it takes to be a man,
Like reaching out to those less blessed
And extend'n a helping hand.

And I hope that day, when my time comes,
I'll ride that trail you rode,
The one that leads to heaven,
The one that's paved with gold.

We'll both be up there horseback
And I'll listen once again,
To the stories of a time gone by,
Just me and my ol' friend.

29

Here's to the Cowboy Life

It weren't much of a life, so some folks say,
But I wouldn't 've had it any other way.
Push'n cows and getting dirty
I reckon it didn't look too purty
Ridin' drag and fixin' fence,
Sometimes it didn't make much sense.

But the good Lord let me make my choice.
On a quiet prairie I could hear his voice.
He showed me mountains that glittered gold
And clear blue lakes of icy cold,
Eagles fly'n in the air
And bear cubs play'n without a care.

I've seen blistering days and cold winter nights,
A calf being born and barroom fights,
Prairie grass a gently waving,
Wolf pups in the meadows misbehav'n,
Longhorns walk'n single file,
They'd be stretched out for at least a mile.

It weren't all fun, there were pain and tears,
Like when I lost that ol' mare I'd had for years.
She was purty ornery when I broke her to ride
And it broke my heart when she finally died.
There were times she was my only friend,
But at the Rainbow Bridge we'll ride again.

I gonna miss the smell of campfire smoke,
So thick that it would make ya choke.
With mesquite embers a glowing bright
As the morning turned from dark to light.
With coffee on the coals and beans a burn'n
And the smell of bacon need'n turn'n.

But this cowboy life, truth be told,
Will take a young man and make him old.
With open range for a bunk house and the prairie
for a bed,
A starry sky for a blanket and a saddle for my
head.
I've seen it all, both bad and good,
I'd do it all again, if only I could.

So here's to all the trails that we've been on,
To all the hands that have come and gone,
To all the ponies we broke and rode,
And all the times that we got throw'd,
Here's to all the glory and the strife,
Here's to all the boys and the cowboy life.

Into The Setting Sun

He stood there like a king,
So strong and straight and tall.
He saw the hawk above the clouds
And listened to his call.

He felt the breeze against his back,
He smelled the sage so sweet.
He knew his friend would be there soon,
The morning they would greet.

He felt the reins across his neck,
The saddle on his back.
As his old friend cinched it down
And took up all the slack.

He stood there with his head held high,
His best friend at his side.
He sensed excitement in the air
For today they're going to ride.

With every hill they climbed
And every stream they crossed,
Their bond kept getting stronger
With a trust that would never be lost.

They knew each other's every mood,
They came to ride as one.
It seemed they'd ride forever
Into the setting sun.

As the years passed by, they both slowed down,
The trot became a walk.
They'd stop to rest more often now,
His horse could barely see the hawk.

And then one day his eyes grew dim,
And in his heart he wanted to ride,
But he just stood there in his stall
With his old friend at his side.

He had to lay him down today,
The hardest thing he's ever done.
But in another time and place they'll ride
Into the setting sun.

Open Ranges of My Mind

I'm just an old cowboy
Who has seen better days.
But once a cowboy, always a cowboy,
In so many ways.

I may not buckaroo
Like I did long ago,
But it's all I ever wanted
And I think you should know.

It was the horse and the saddle
That drew me as a boy
And my heroes on TV
Like Hoppy and Roy.

I dreamt when I was young
And it may sound strange,
Of push'n cows up the trail
And across open range.

But move'n cattle on feed lots
Was as close as I got.
But I didn't mind much
And it sure weren't for not.

'Cause I finally saved enough
To buy that little spread,
'Bout a hundred acres
I bought from ol' Ned.

It weren't noth'n to brag on,
But it sure was all mine
And I recall that little boy
And his dreams from time to time.

With my bandana of silk
And the boots on my feet,
I'd grab hold of them reins
And take a deep seat.

I'd close my eyes tight
And here's what I saw
That scene from "Red River"
When they all yelled, YEEHAW!

At the start of the drive
When they were all head'n out,
They'd all wave their hats
And would holler and shout.

And dern, if I don't get
Just as big of a thrill
Just move'n those cows
Back over the hill.

But to this very day
I'm still play'n pretend
And follow'n that trail
To the very end.

It really don't matter
Which trail you choose,
'Cause sometimes ya win
And sometimes ya lose.

But being a cowboy
Means following your dreams
And staying true to yourself,
No matter how tough life seems.

Even if that range
Is just in my mind,
I'm live'n my dream
And do'n just fine.

Saddle Dreams

I can't remember the last time I took a deep seat
And rode my ol' horse just for fun.
It seems like every time I saddle up,
There's a passel of work to be done.

Like sort'n or pen'n or fix'n a post,
Or stretch'n some wire tight
Or learn'n your mare is throw'n her colt
And hav'n to stay up all night.

Don't get me wrong, I love this life.
A cowboy's all I ever wanted to be.
But just once in awhile, I'd like to take some time
And ride out just for me.

Now I've heard it said, time again,
A fellow should stop and smell the flowers,
But the scent I get is the backside of a cow
And it seems to linger for hours.

To sit in my saddle
And watch a hawk fly overhead
Or hear coyote pups a howling
While they feast on something dead.

It's the little things like these
That bring a smile to my face,
And I could purely enjoy them
If it weren't for the hectic pace.

Well, today's gonna be different,
I'm gonna lie here in my bed
And just for a moment
Ponder the day ahead.

I'll take my time
Greet'n the day.
I'll skip mucking the stalls
And rake'n the hay.

I'll have a second cup of coffee,
Then saddle up ol' Joe.
We'll most likely start the day off
With no particular place to go.

We might head out
Towards them hills to the west
Or south to the lake
Where the fish'n is best.

It don't really matter
Which direction we go,
'Cause where we'll end up,
We don't really know.

We'll just take our sweet time
And breathe in the air.
We'll ride some ol' trail
Like we don't have a care.

Just ride'n out
Enjoying the bliss.
Life just don't get
Any better than this.

But all of a sudden
I hear a sound!
It's my alarm goin' off,
As my feet hit the ground.

It's still dark outside
So I didn't sleep late.
Thank the Lord for sure
For jerk'n me awake.

So now it's back up,
'Cause there's work to be done.
It was nice while it lasted
And it would have been fun.

I'd sure like to go
At least that's how it seems
On another long ride
With those sweet saddle dreams.

Prairie Fire (Lost Love)

I was work'n on the ol' Bar C
Back in '59,
Push'n horns from here to there
With this young cowboy friend of mine.

We was just a ride'n
With our ponies' heads too low,
He turns to me and says,
I got a question for ya, Joe.

Have ya ever been in love?
I thought I heard him say.
I tried my best to ignore him
As I looked the other way.

I ain't talk'n about the honky tonk'n
Two shot type of love.
I mean the can't eat, can't sleep,
Sent from heaven up above.

Well, I could tell right then and there
This would be one of those days
I'd wished I stayed inside the barn
With my horse a eat'n hay.

Well, I thought and I pondered
On that subject for awhile
Then it started come'n back to me
And I couldn't help but smile.

Like little snap shots from my past
Tucked far back in my mind,
I could see her standing there
With her face so soft and kind.

Yes sir, I said, there was a time
Many years ago
I met the woman of my dreams,
But then I let her go.

I saw her red hair flow'n
Like a wild prairie fire.
It was at that very moment
She became my heart's desire.

As I just sat there horseback,
I could hear the pound'n of my heart.
I wanted so to speak to her,
But I didn't know where to start.

And then she turned and looked up at me
From the corners of her eyes.
She smiled and said, good mornin sir,
Much to my surprise.

I tried so hard to say hello,
But I was trip'n on my tongue.
I guess that's just the price you pay,
For being shy and being young.

She'd been out there pick'n wild flowers,
They grew as far as you could see.
She said this one is just for you
As she handed it to me.

There weren't no way I'd ever want
That flower to be hurt.
So I wrapped it in my kerchief
And placed it gently in my shirt.

I finally got a few words out.
I had no idea as what to say.
But we sat there on the prairie
For the best part of the day.

She spoke of things of beauty
And places she'd like to go.
She had a gypsy's spirit,
But displayed a gentle soul.

She said I really must be going,
We're leaving here today.
I just came out to pick these flowers
To pass them out along the way.

So others can see what I have seen
And the beauty that is here,
And so I may never forget
This place I hold so dear.

Will we ever meet again? I asked.
She said, I'm afraid we never will.
Then she turned and walked away
Head'n back over the hill.

With the set'n sun behind her,
Her silhouette against the sky,
Red hair a blowing in the breeze,
I knew I had to say goodbye.

I watched her in the distance
Until she faded from my sight,
But like my little prairie fire,
My love won't vanish in the night.

It sure didn't matter much
That I never knew her name.
It didn't matter whatsoever,
I loved her just the same.

Why didn't you go after her
When she went back over the hill?
She could have been your one true love,
You could've been with her still.

She was, she is, my one true love,
She's been with me all these years.
She held me when I was happy
And wiped away my tears.

I've had my share of ladies,
On that you can be sure,
But I've only loved one woman
With a love that's real and pure.

I'm a cowboy and a drifter,
I knew I'd never settle down.
She's been right here in my heart
At every ranch and every town.

Thank you for reminding me
Of the love I've held so dear.
I guess it's finally time to ride on back
And get ourselves a beer.

Behind the Poems

Whenever I'm reciting my poetry, whether it's around a campfire, at a festival or gathering, or just with some friends getting together, someone always seems to ask, where did you get the idea for this poem or that poem. And after reading other poets over the last fifty plus years, give or take, I have sometimes wondered where their ideas came from as well. So I thought it might be kind of fun to share with you the stories behind a few of the poems in <u>Buckaroo Poetry</u>. The themes come from every day life, and like many poets, I try to tell a simple story that others can relate to.

Wanda Jean and Me

This poem is as close to the truth as you can get and I have always wanted to share her story. So in a way this book is a tribute to her. I rescued Wanda Jean in 2000. She had been abandoned. She was pastured in an area that had a broken down arena and the remnant of a corral in total disarray. She was skinny, barefoot and her hooves were way over due. She had been penned up for some time with no attention. I was halfway looking for a new horse, when a friend told me about her. I went over to have a look. She wouldn't have anything to do with me. Even a carrot didn't help. I just wrote it off to her being an Appy mare and having a bad attitude. Well, she threw down the gauntlet and I picked it up and the rest is pretty much as it is written. She turned out to be a great girl who got me out of more than one jam. I always said, she was a better horse than I was a rider. She passed away on December 27, 2011 with her head on my lap and I wrote the poem that night.

Ol' 519

What cowboy, young or old, has not gone to a rodeo and come away thinking, I wish I could try that just once. It's that little buckaroo down deep inside of all of us that refuses to grow up and he always shows up at rodeo time. Driving back from a PBR event last year, I told my wife how I'd wished I had tried bull riding just once, before I got too old. She said I was too old and the closest I would ever get was writing about it. That's when the wheels started turning on Ol' 519.

The Old Man's Ranch

Cowboy poetry and storytelling are really just about life in general. Everyone needs to survive the hard winter, just like they welcome the mild summer. It's how we find balance on the trail of life. My father passed away several years back, due to complications to Alzheimer's. I wanted to take a few lines and pay tribute to my father and all of the millions of families who are affected by Alzheimer's disease and other forms of dementia.

Buckaroo Heaven

I believe that every boy has an Ol' Ned in their life. It may be a grandfather, an older uncle or a family friend. Back in the early 1950's, I had a neighbor. I always referred to him as Mr. Johnson because back then we were never allowed to call grown-ups by their first name. Anything else was considered disrespectful. I used to go over and visit him when my chores were done. He was born about 1880 and he would sit on a log stump and tell me stories of when he was a young fellow. Mr. Johnson would go on about right and wrong and how a man was judged by his character and his word. He talked about helping others less fortunate and about heaven as if it were a resort he had always wanted to visit. He could paint a picture with his words. My old friend passed away after I went in the Army in 1963. I miss him.

Here's to the Cowboy Life

This one I wrote for all the hard working cattle ranchers I have had the privilege of knowing, the unsung heroes of the cowboy world. There's no glitter and no gold. It's sun up to sun down. You don't work, you don't eat. It's a real simple equation, but one of the most complicated life styles that has ever been. You have to be an expert on the land, the water, the livestock, grain, feed, machinery, weather, construction, horsemanship, fixing fences and posts, and birthing calves, and then you still have to find time to help raise a family and go to church on Sunday. This one is dedicated to all the fine folks in the Ventura County Cattleman's Association. You won't find more dedicated people anywhere.

Into The Setting Sun

This poem I wrote for my trail buddy, good friend and author, Jim Christina. He had this big old Appaloosa that could get you down any trail, anywhere, anytime. Roseman, as Jim called him, was the most gentle horse I ever knew. Sadly, he developed moon blindness. We doctored him for almost a year. He knew we were trying to help him, but despite our efforts, he lost his battle. Every cowboy loves a good horse, whether it's yours or your pal's. After Jim had to put him down, I wrote this in honor of The Roseman.

Well, now you know where a few of my poems came from. I suggest if you have an idea, just put pen to paper and see what comes of it. You'll be surprised how much fun it is. Sometimes, when you're feeling down, it's just the thing to get you over some rocky trail.

Thank you for stopping by.
P.W. Conway

Made in the USA
Middletown, DE
03 March 2015